Snow White
and the
Seven Dwarfs

MW01701299

Illustrated by Dorothea King

GONDOLA

Once there was a little princess called Snow White. Her stepmother was a wicked Queen. The Queen was very beautiful. Every day she looked into her magic mirror and said,

"Mirror, mirror on the wall,
Who is the fairest of them all?"

Every day the mirror would reply,

"You, oh Queen, are the fairest in all the land."

One day the Queen asked,
"Mirror, mirror on the wall,
Who is the fairest of them all?"
And the mirror replied,
"You, oh Queen, are very fair,
But Snow White is the fairest
in all the land."
Instead of seeing her own face in
the mirror the Queen saw the face
of Snow White. She was very angry.

The Queen sent for her huntsman.
''Take Snow White into the forest
and kill her,'' she said.
The huntsman loved Snow White.
''I cannot kill you,'' he said
taking Snow White into the forest.
''But you cannot go home.
You must stay in the forest.''
The huntsman returned to the
palace alone. He told the Queen
he had killed Snow White.

Snow White wandered alone through
the dark forest. She came to
a little house.
"Perhaps the people who live here
will help me," she said.
She knocked at the door.
There was no reply, so she peeped
inside. It was a very untidy
house. Everything in it was very
small. There was seven of
everything – seven chairs, seven
spoons, seven mugs and seven plates.

Snow White was so hungry she ate some bread from the table. Then she said, "I will tidy up for the people who live here." She swept and dusted, cleaned and polished. She had plenty of helpers. Then, because she was tired she lay on one of the seven beds and fell fast asleep.

The cottage was lived in by seven dwarfs. They worked in a mine on the far side of the forest.
When they got home they found Snow White asleep. Snow White woke up with a start.
"Who . . . who are you?" she asked.
"This is our house," said the dwarfs. "Do not be afraid, we will not hurt you, but tell us what you are doing here."

Snow White told the dwarfs what had happened.
"You can stay here and we will look after you," said the dwarfs.
Snow White and the dwarfs lived happily together. But the dwarfs were afraid the wicked Queen would come looking for Snow White. They told her not to open the door to anyone. They were right to be worried.

The Queen asked her mirror,
"Mirror, mirror on the wall,
Who is the fairest of them all?"
The mirror replied,
"You, oh Queen, are very fair,
But Snow White who lives in the
forest with the little men,
is the fairest in all the land."
The Queen was very angry.
"I will kill Snow White myself,"
she said.

The Queen dressed herself as a pedlar. She filled a basket with apples then went into the forest. She waited until the dwarfs had gone to the mine, then she knocked at the door of the little house.

"I have nothing to fear from a pedlar," said Snow White. And she opened the door.

"Good day, child," said the Queen.
"Would you like one of my apples?"
"Oh, yes please . . ." said Snow White.
The Queen gave Snow White the
reddest apple in the basket.
It was a very special apple.
The Queen had put a spell on it.
"Take a bite . . ." said the Queen.

Snow White took one bite from the apple and fell to the ground.
"Ha! Ha!" laughed the Queen.
"Snow White is dead. Now I am the fairest in all the land."
When the dwarfs came home, they found Snow White lying on the ground. The apple was lying beside her.
"The wicked Queen has been here," they said sadly. "Snow White is dead."

The dwarfs built a special bed for Snow White in the forest. The animals kept watch around her. One day a Prince came riding by and saw Snow White lying there. "Please let me take her home." he said. As the Prince lifted Snow White onto his horse she opened her eyes. The piece of magic apple had fallen from her throat.

''Snow White is alive!'' shouted the dwarfs. ''Hoorah! Hoorah!'' Once more the Queen asked,
''Mirror, mirror on the wall,
Who is the fairest of them all?''
The mirror replied,
''You, oh Queen are very fair,
But Snow White, the Prince's bride is the fairest in all the land.''
The Queen was so angry, she flew into a rage and died. Snow White was safe at last.